THE RESCUE

The daring rescue of seven missionaries against impossible odds

by

Dave Anderson

with Norm Rohrer

Fellowship Publishing
Tempe, Arizona

Scripture taken from the
HOLY BIBLE, NEW INTERNATIONAL VERSION.
© Copyright 1973, 1978, 1984 International Bible Society.
Used by permission of Zondervan Bible Publishers.

ISBN 0-9628303-6-4
Product FP 30357

Fellowship Publishing
6202 S. Maple
Tempe, AZ 85283
(602) 838-8500
(602) 838-9187 fax

Printed in the United States of America

Cover Painting by Ray Martens

Book Design by Mindy Jasmund

*T*O GOD, OUR GREAT DELIVERER

"Where can I go from Your Spirit?
Where can I flee from Your presence?
If I go up to the heavens, You are there;
If I make my bed in the depths, You are there.
If I rise on the wings of the dawn,
If I settle on the far side of the sea,
Even there Your hand will guide me,
Your right hand will hold me fast."

Psalm 139 : 7-10

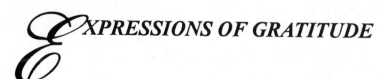

EXPRESSIONS OF GRATITUDE

To Our Rescuers:

Capt. Eric Penttila, Evergreen Helicopter Pilot
Randy Oles, Nome Volunteer Fire Department
Jerry Austin, Evergreen Helicopter Mechanic
Capt. Walter Greaves, ERA Helicopter Pilot
Dave Miles, ERA Geological Survey Team Member
Terry Day, Bering Air Pilot for surveillance
Vic Olson, Baker Aviation Pilot for surveillance
FAA Employees Jay Langton, Val Larson, and Jim Miller
Christopher Brown, Anchorage Air Traffic Controller
and the staff of Nome Flight Service

To the Medical Staff at the
Norton Sound Regional Medical Center

To Local Church Leaders

Pastor Marvin and Janis Eppard-- Nome
Pastor Bill Welch, Nome
Pastor Jim Falsey, Nome
Pastor Richard Creager, Fairbanks

To Hundreds of Others Including:

Bering Sea Women's Group, Nome
Alaska Airlines personnel
Gene and Shirley Moe, Anchorage

Doug Doyel, Nome Fire Department
Mr. and Mrs. Terry Wilson, EMT
...and to all who aided in our rescue

**And to those with whom I will forever
have a special bond...survivors**
My loving wife Barbara, Cary Dietsche, Brian Brasher,
Don Wharton, Pam Swedberg, and Dave Cochran

Special thanks to Elling and Barbara Halvorson of Woodenville, WA
for their help in making this book possible.

ONTENTS

REFACE

Sprawling wide and bleak on the tundra west of the Bering Sea of Alaska, lie Russian villages less than an hour's flight from Nome but culturally world's away. Caressed by fog and battered by the wind, the sore and blistered buildings of Provideniya and Lavrentiya stand gray and stark on the barren, treeless land of the Chukotka Peninsula. *The National Geographic* reported that Provideniya, home to 5,000 Russian people, looks like a bombed-out ghost town, "a town that had declared war on itself and won." Lavrentiya, a 45-minute flight to the north, is equally depressed and lacking in amenities such as entertainment and modern conveniences, and more importantly, employment opportunities. There is no church there and Bibles are scarce.

In the 70 years from the Communist revolution right up to 1990, the Russians in these remote cities maintained the far eastern listening post for a government dedicated to the destruction of the United States of America. Communist soldiers who volunteered for duty in this ultramundane military post were paid $150 per month, three times more than workers in Moscow 6,500 miles to the west.

With steady propaganda and rigid indoctrination, the Soviet government made certain that none of the people on the Bering Sea found out that life was better in America on the other side of the sea. No Russian was allowed to own a boat lest he try to leave the hard conditions of Lenin's "utopia". Radios were rigged so that they could receive signals only from Communist stations, nothing from the West. There are no highways or railroads leading out of either town. With such restraints, how were these citizens ever to hear the Gospel of Jesus Christ unless someone were to tell them? God answered that question by inspiring Christian believers in Alaska to be first to cross the water with the Good News.

In 1993 my wife Barbara and I, as part of our ministry for Christ and His Kingdom through music carried out by The Fellowship Ministries headquartered in Tempe, Arizona, felt called by God to return to Alaska and preach the gospel through music. This time missionary Dick Page at M.A.R.C. (Missionary Aviation and Repair Center) suggested that we consider carrying out our mission in newly opened Lavrentiya, a little over an hour's flight from Nome. We agreed to pray about the matter and began to gather our team.

We invited our full-time keyboardist Cary Dietsche, road manager Brian Brasher, and special guest, singer/songwriter Don Wharton. Enthusiasm for the trip to Lavrentiya began running high and much prayer ascended to God for His direction.

Through M.A.R.C.'s contacts, our team was joined for their mission by 18 teenagers and adults from a church in Soldotna, Alaska on the Kenai Peninsula who were ready and eager to fly to Lavrentiya with food and medicine, and to participate in our evangelistic outreach.

The night before Barb and I left Phoenix, several friends and neighbors helped to repackage hundreds of pounds of medicines donated by area clinics in the States. The gifts were to be given to Lavrentiya's clinics and hospital. We little realized then that our trip home from the remote city of Russia would cost us all of our possessions and take us to the door of death. But today we all declare with the Apostle Paul,

"None of these things move me; nor do I count my life dear to myself so that I may finish my race with joy, and the ministry which I received from the Lord Jesus, to testify to the gospel of the grace of God."

--Acts 20:24

THE RESCUE

but those who hope in the LORD will renew their strength.
They will soar on wings like eagles;
they will run and not grow weary,
they will walk and not be faint.

Isaiah 40:31

0323:41	ZAN	*"November Six Sierra Foxtrot, are you declaring an emergency?"*
0323:46	N6SF	*"Yes...please. I'm about two miles short of Sledge Island."*
0323:48	ZAN R3	*"Say how many souls onboard."*
0323:49	N6SF	*"Seven."*
0323:51	ZAN R3	*"All right northwest sixty-nine. Roger. Standby please, November six sierra foxtrot. Understand you are two miles short of Sledge Island now?"*
0324:05	N6SF	....
0324:17	ZAN	*"November six sierra foxtrot transmission was clipped..."*

CHAPTER ONE

Like a Mighty Army

CHAPTER ONE

Like a Mighty Army

*L*ate in 1992, I placed a phone call to Dick Page, Assistant Director of Missionary Aviation and Repair Center (M.A.R.C.) in Soldotna, Alaska, to lay plans for a return to Alaska. On previous trips to "The Last Frontier," We had sung the gospel in towns with such unlikely names as Unalakleet, Shishmaref, and Shaktoolik. We had grown to love the Eskimos. Our hearts were warmed by their openness to the gospel and by their love of Christian music.

I asked the Alaska pilot if M.A.R.C. would be interested in helping to organize a ministry tour in Eskimo villages as the organization had done before, flying us from village to village in one of their airplanes.

"Yes," said Dick, "we can do that." Then, after a pause, he made a suggestion: "But why don't you and Barb think about letting us take you to Russia instead."

The forbidden land of our former enemy? Little more than an hour's flight toward the setting sun? Why not?

M.A.R.C. had initiated the first flight to Lavrentiya and Provideniya on the western side of the Bering Strait. Dick Page was certain that our ministry through music would be effective in presenting the gospel to those Russian communities.

The 'Siberia Mission'

We began to pray earnestly, seeking to ascertain God's will about a trip to Russia. We talked with our pastor, with trusted friends, and with other musicians about an evangelistic thrust we called "Siberia Mission." Only after putting "Siberia" in our mission's title did we discover that the Siberian border was actually 2,000 miles west of this barren area of the world's largest country. Of course, the Soviet Union had changed names since Mikhail Gorbachev supervised the dissolution of the empire which was now called the "Commonwealth of Independent States" (C.I.S.). Oh well, somehow "Siberia" fit that lonely peninsula best so the name for the mission stuck.

"God bless your mission in Siberia," friends in many areas of the United States began writing, enclosing gifts and promising to pray.

The Family of Christ Church of Phoenix, in which we have our membership, pledged $500 toward the trip. Another $500 was donated by individual members. Gifts from the Aid Association to Lutherans and from Lutheran Brotherhood branches arrived, joined by gifts from Sunday schools and women's groups for "Siberia Mission."

One day we received a letter from ministry friends in Houston, Texas, asking if our group planned to take Bibles along to Russia. "Yes," we wrote back, "but raising travel funds for our evangelistic mission is our priority for this trip. We'll purchase Russian Bibles with any extra funds that are donated."

Two weeks later our friends in Texas sent a check for $4,000 designating that $1,800 of that amount be used for the purchase of Bibles. By mid-summer of 1993, The Fellowship Ministries had raised enough money to take along 300 copies of the most sought-after book in Russia--the Holy Bible. Each copy was fully illustrated in color and published in Russian by the Slavic Gospel Association.

'Here am I...'

The first member of the team to be invited was guitarist and singer/songwriter Don Wharton from Nashville, a friend of many years. We like his down-home sense of humor, and knew it would add warmth and humor to the concerts.

A member of the Lutheran Laymans League's Medical Committee donated several hundred pounds of medical supplies, to which were added gifts from the Thomas Davis Medical Center in Phoenix and from Project C.U.R.E. in Denver. We missionaries ended up with 1,000 pounds of medical supplies for the inhabitants of "Siberia".

In July 1993, several weeks before our "Siberia Mission" team departed, we received word that 18 adults and young people in Alaska, most of them members from Soldotna Bible Chapel and the Missionary Aviation and Repair Center, planned to accompany us to Russia. These Alaska Christians wanted to join us in this ministry to their Russian neighbors. They had purchased 3,000 pounds of food to be flown to Lavrentiya for their "neighbors" across the sea. The shipment contained bananas, oranges, apples, onions, carrots, potatoes, garlic, and green peppers, along with several 40-pound bags of rice, flour and sugar. Just as the brethren of long ago distributed "the daily ministrations" among those who were neglected, so the modern Christians added the "serving of tables" to their gospel itinerary in Russia with the provision of coveted staples.

Departure Day arrived. We gathered with friends for one final prayer in Phoenix's Sky Harbor Airport then rose on the wings of the wind in a jet toward Seattle, thence to Anchorage where we joined our fellow believers in Soldotna on the Kenai Peninsula south of Anchorage. Next day we flew to remote Nome just below the Arctic Circle aboard three M.A.R.C. planes--a Cessna 310 and two Piper Navajos.

Two hours later as we circled over Norton Sound on our approach to the landing strip at Nome we could see off to the west the smoky waters of the Bering Strait. Who could have imagined that within a few days we would be floundering for our lives in that watery tomb.

We transferred our musical instruments, keyboard, sound equipment and all the cargo of our mercy mission to a cream colored twin-engine PA 31/A Piper Navajo which M.A.R.C. had rented from Lake Clark Air for pilot Dave Olson with Mission Aviation Fellowship. As I climbed aboard that airplane I thought of a phone call from Valerie

Bullock which had come two weeks before we left Arizona. She had attended our concert at a Lutheran Church in Holyoke, Colorado and heard about our trip to Alaska.

"While you were singing," she said, "I had a vision."
"Of what?" I asked apprehensively. "Well, I saw your plane fall out of the sky over the ocean near Alaska... you crashed... and...and [her voice became a whisper] you all died."

As I was pondering her words she continued: "I'm not saying that I know where this vision came from." I asked if she had ever had a vision before. "Yes," she said slowly. "And it came true."

I thanked her for phoning and prayed with her before hanging up. I committed the entire matter to the Lord and went forward anyway with our plans for the "Siberian Mission."

I paused another moment and looked at that long, sleek piece of machinery. Its engines were powerful, its workings well maintained. Barb and I committed the journey to the Lord, strapped ourselves in and soon were aloft, streaking toward Russia, watching our country disappear under the wing as a tip of the 6,592,000 square miles of the Russian Federation approached.

After a little more than an hour in the air, the long, low gray buildings of Provideniya, the official point of entry, appeared on the horizon. Only a few years earlier, that scene would have struck fear in the heart of an American because the declared purpose of the city was to crush the Yankee warlords who, they feared, were bent on destroying them. Once hundreds of thousands of Soviet soldiers were bivouacked at Provideniya 6,200 miles from Moscow. Their guns were aimed at America, their listening devices trained on the United States. When America invaded, they were told, Russians needed to be there to defend the Motherland. In this sterile environment the temperature almost warms up four months of the year and here winters are dark and extremely cold. When the sun shone, the people were happy; when clouds appeared and the bleak chill descended, the people withdrew and an oppression seemed to settle on them. We missionaries had come to bring the people not only material blessings but also the Light of Life.

I love you, O Lord, my strength.
The Lord is my rock, my fortress and my deliver,
my God is my rock, in whom I take refuge.
He is my shield and the horn of my salvation, my stronghold.
I call to the LORD, who is worthy of praise,
and I am saved from my enemies.
The cords of death entangled me;
the torrents of destruction overwhelmed me.
The cords of the grave coiled around me;
the snares of death confronted me.
In my distress I called to the LORD;
I cried to my God for help.
From his temple he heard my voice;
my cry came before Him, into His ears.
The earth trembled and quaked ,
and the foundations of the mountains shook; they trembled because He was angry.
Smoke rose from His nostrils; consuming fire came from His mouth,
burning coals blazed out of it.
He parted the heavens and came down;
dark clouds were under His feet.
He mounted the cherubim and flew;
He soared on the wings of the wind.
He made darkness His covering, His canopy around Him-
the dark rain clouds of the sky.

Psalm 18 : 1-11

CHAPTER TWO

Christ is Born Across the Sea

CHAPTER TWO

Christ is Born Across the Sea

Our plane settled like an eagle on the sprawling, primitive military gravel runway and taxied up to shabby buildings that served as customs for the Provideniya Airport. We were followed by three other planes in our contingent--another Piper Navajo, one Cessna 310 and one Sky Master. We all waited in our cockpits for the official greeting and an invitation to unload our possessions for customs inspection. We cringed when a gangly old Russian military flatbed truck rumbled up to our plane and two workers began offloading our precious cargo. Then the truck rattled away to an opening in the wall of the airport building. All of our expensive sound equipment, personal items, medicine, food, and other cargo were handed through a hole in the wall to be claimed later.

We all presented our passports then retrieved our items from the truck and sat down in the outer hall of the customs building to wait for the processing. We felt intimidated by two guards who watched our every move. I shiver when I think of that room. Its floor was made of cracked ceramic tiles, adding a stark motif to the unheated room. We all felt fearful and unsure. With Psalm 89:1 in mind, we decided to gather in a circle and sing. Our music chased the gloom and seemed to open the windows of heaven. The guards relaxed and grinned. Overhead the sun peeked from behind dark clouds as if to show God's approval of our "concert". But quickly the steel sky returned and the relentless fog began to settle on us. I feared that we would be stuck in that ungarnished place until the sunrise and so I began to pray. My only thoughts were: *Let's get out of this place and get on to Lavrentiya!*

Provideniya was named by a Danish explorer, Vitrus Bering, back in the 1700s. Captain Bering and his crew were caught in a ferocious storm. When it looked as though their ship would certainly go down with all lives lost, Captain Bering cried, "If there is a Providence, save our lives!" Almost as soon as that prayer left his lips, his ship was swept into a quiet bay which is now the site of Provideniya ("Providence"). How ironic it is that despite such a dramatic history, the residents all these years have been told that there is no Providence!

I wandered about the customs facility a bit, greeting soldiers, inspecting their quarters and even sniffing the tempting fish soup in the dining room of the airport terminal. Barb was more timid, preferring to stay put and wait politely for the cue to fly on to our destination. We offered small treats to the guards and then heard the good news: Our 45-minute flight to Lavrentiya was approved. As we climbed aboard, Dave Olson checked his instruments, studied his map and then started the engines. Soon we were racing with throttle up down that gravel runway then up, up, up over the mountains, bays and inlets of the Chukotka Peninsula northbound to the farthest point in the Russia Federation. I think every member of the team in our plane and in three other planes following us felt relieved and inspired as we headed toward Lavrentiya.

Missionary Wally Kulakoff of World Radio Missionary Fellowship based in Quito, Ecuador, was able to join our group as main interpreter and was riding in our plane to Lavrentiya. Wally was born in China of Russian parents while they were fleeing to Australia from Red armies which slaughtered millions of Christian believers. Our brother, Mr. Kulakoff, currently directs the Russian language programming for HCJB Radio which beams the Gospel in 28 languages from Quito. He holds Australian citizenship and speaks fluent Russian and Spanish, as well as English. As we flew at 1,500 feet above the rugged coastline, Wally entertained us with stories about the people to whom we were taking music, medicine, food, Bibles and tracts in the name of the Lord Jesus Christ. He prayed that because of our efforts, a permanent work could be established in Lavrentiya.

At the End of the World

Lavrentiya is a coastal town of approximately 4,000 people. It was settled approximately 70 years ago as a military base because the Communists were convinced that American forces would invade their country. Lavrentiyans were taught that Americans were the enemy, that Americans were all poor and hungry, that life was harsh in the United States and that life for Communists was easy by comparison. Just knowing that Lavrentiya's listening posts and electronic eavesdropping were operational enabled other Russian citizens to feel secure. The coming of <u>Peristroika</u> and <u>Glasnost</u> made Lavrentiya obsolete as a listening post. Wally translated a huge piece of writing on the side of a mountain which said, *"Slava Sovetskim Pogranichnikam!"* (Glory to the Soviet Border Guards.) We laughed as we looked from the sign to the eroding buildings and the deserted lookout posts facing Alaska and remembered the confused border patrol officers guarding our small plane. It was historic that three small American planes flew from Provideniya to Lavrentiya without a Russian co-pilot.

Why was the city still there? Because there was nowhere else for the people to go. It was home to the residents--stark, lonely and cold, but "home" nevertheless.

The airstrip had been built right through the middle of town, as if to give citizens a front-row seat to every military or commercial plane taking off and landing. Our MAF Pilot, Dave Olson, set N6SF down on the runway, taxied to a parking spot and shut off the engines. We scrambled off and watched as three other planes in our contingent landed behind us. The army of the Lord had arrived. Great things were going to happen.

In minutes we were surrounded by a welcoming delegation of city officials. Behind them came the ubiquitous Russian flatbed truck in search of cargo which it transferred to the town's "White House" (the seat of local and area governments) across from the Cultural Center less than a block away from where our nightly meetings were to be held. A large room in this building served as our headquarters for the four days we would be in Lavrentiya.

In the welcoming committee was Alexi Astapov, a former agent of the KGB who, a few years earlier, might have had us all under arrest and locked in the hoosegow for questioning. But we had no secrets. We were just a group of Americans who were followers of the Lord Jesus Christ, come to offer gifts, to sing the praises of our Savior, and to invite people to reach out and touch Him by faith.

'Take me! Take me!'

One of the Russians who responded warmly was German (pronounced Gear-mon) Volnov, Jr., a young man ordered by officials to keep an eye on us. His name meant "Little German" and he showed signs of deep conviction when he heard the messages of Salvation. We grew to love Little German and his wife, Yana. There were indications that their feelings were mutual. Joining the entourage with Little German, Yana and Alexi were dozens of children who tagged along for the show. They appeared at the windows, clogged the entrances to buildings and relished our gifts. We could count on these enthusiastic children to line up for the gospel meetings in the evenings after supper.

I confided to our team, "If a Russian-speaking person would start a ministry to children in Lavrentiya that person could bring an entire generation of young Russians into the family of Jesus Christ." The prospect became a subject for prayer.

One evening during our program Don Wharton looked at four rows of approximately 50 children sitting in the audience, spread his arms and exclaimed, "I wish I could take you all home with me." The moment Don's words were translated by Wally Kulakoff dozens of the children shouted in Russian, *"Vozmitye menya! Vozmitye menya!"* ("Take me! Take me!").

Strange New World

We all agreed that Lavrentiya is "one of the most depressing places we've ever seen." Perhaps it was not as bad as crowded Calcutta. No one was starving. Dead bodies were not lying in the street. Outdoor cooking fumes and the scent of diesel fuel do not fill the streets. However, Lavrentiya is more remote, just as desperate in its loneliness, just as lacking in fulfilling careers and totally without the tender associations of the Church.

Streets of Lavrentiya are dusty and dirty. Every slab of concrete is badly cracked and broken. Above-ground "housing" for the town's central heating system urgently needs repair. Russians and Eskimos inhabit buildings that appear to be uninhabitable. Trash clutters every corner, including piles of rusted-out engine hulks and obsolete equipment. We thought the stray dogs were "kind of cute," but they were everywhere and sometimes annoying and ominous. The softening of green grass landscaping was absent. Even in the "heat" of summer only a few flowering weeds and not a single tree could be found anywhere. Any planted tree would soon be victimized by icy winds off the Bering Sea.

As we struggled to become acclimated to the strange new unkempt world we awaited with a degree of apprehension the assignments to our guest quarters. A young woman approached Barb and me, introducing herself as Irena, the daughter of the couple who would be our hosts. She led us down an ungarnished and weathered street to one of many bleak, six-story concrete apartment buildings. Its wooden front door hung precariously on its hinges, eaten by decay and weathered by a hundred seasons. Stairwells were bare cement and darkly lit. We began to wonder what the interior would be like.

Irena motioned for us to follow as she scampered up two floors where she knocked on one of the doors. No one answered, but this resourceful little lady had a key and she let us in. It was obvious to us that Irena was upset because her mother was not at home but we tried to assure her that we didn't mind waiting.

In the tiny but orderly quarters, Irena offered us hot tea from a lovely porcelain tea pot which she poured into delicate porcelain cups painted with roses. With delicious tea she served freshly baked bread which was as good as any we've ever eaten. We learned later that this bread was a staple food of the community, baked three times a day in a central bakery and available for sale in time for each meal. During these times it was not uncommon to see Lavrentiyans walking from the local bakery to their dwellings carrying unwrapped loaves or packaged bread--all of it with an aroma that made your mouth water. Bread is a staple, and so is salty, orange salmon caviar. Drying mushrooms were strung on thread from the kitchen ceiling.

Soon Irena's mother, Marguerite, returned, breathless and embarrassed for having been absent when the Americans arrived. She had hurried across the tundra after a day of picking fresh blueberries, carrying the precious booty in a big white bucket. She quickly excused herself and disappeared into her kitchen to prepare a bowl for Barb and me. Marguerite was an Eskimo; her husband, a Russian. Our hostess spoke a few words of English but her husband spoke none. For the week of their visit, we were able to communicate quite well, thanks to the eloquence of sign language.

The walls of Marguerite's home were lined with hundreds of books, several pictures, beautiful ivory carvings and other mementoes. The double bed in our room was comfortable. A small bathroom nearby with a tiny sink, a tub and shower were quite adequate. Several clotheslines hung over the bathtub and there were metal wash tubs across from the sink. Nobody owned a washer or dryer in Lavrentiya. Heating plants serving apartment buildings were unable to regulate their supply. Those apartments nearest the power plant receive the most heat; those farthest away are colder. We were thankful to be near the power plant with enough warm water for our baths and enough heat to keep our room warm for sleeping at night.

In our apartment the toilet was behind a small door in a little room beside the bathroom. The commode was supplied with a small amount of brownish water entering through pipes exposed in the wall behind it. Next to it sat a paper bag into which went all paper waste of any kind.

Our hostess gifts--facial tissue and toilet paper--were eagerly and gratefully received. The cost for board and room was $15 a day, and the board was great. We had reindeer, salmon--smoked, baked, boiled, fried or in soups with rice, eggs and lots of caviar--pink and salty salmon eggs, always washed down by strong tea.

At each meal, when we respectfully asked if we might offer a prayer of thanksgiving, our hosts always left the room. On the night before we left, we returned late after the evening service to find Marguerite seated in her kitchen reading the Russian Bible we had given her. On the morning of our departure, Marguerite remained at the table during prayer.

Inside the door of the White House which contained the room that was headquarters for the group, a large Russian woman was posted as a guard. Barb showed this woman the Russian Bible which she had tucked away to take back to friends in America, whose gift made the Bible purchase possible. The guard was excited to see it and began at once to read it. Barb realized instantly that this copy of God's Word belonged with our guard, not as a souvenir for the Christian friends back home. We both prayed that it would lead to her salvation. When she told the guard the Bible was hers the woman was overwhelmed by emotion. She pressed the Bible to her breast and began to cry. Then she hugged Barb. We gave thanks to God! That Bible obviously was going to be read, and hopefully believed.

Lean Aisles in the Ruble Mart

Lavrentiya's markets were nearly bare. A single dilapidated ill-functioning meat refrigerator struggled to cool two whole chickens completely defeathered (sprouting a few hairs) with necks and legs and feet still intact. It also housed a couple of slabs of meat (probably reindeer steak) a few eggs and nothing else. The shelves yielded a few tins of packaged food, some onions, capped jars of brownish liquid which we learned was fruit juice, a few housewares but not much else. Our hearts ached as we compared the brightly-lit, attractive, well stocked supermarkets back home offering such an abundance of fruits and vegetables, dairy products, bakery goods and a thousand items for creature comforts available at prices the poorest American can afford.

We looked at full-length fur coats in one store. From a distance the coats appeared to be made out of fox fur. When we stroked them, the sensation seemed familiar. Indeed, we knew where we had felt it many times before when the employee told us the coats were made of dog fur.

In the White House basement, I found hundreds of rotting, hardcover books stored in boxes. Every single book is now obsolete propaganda. This kind of material occupied nearly 50% of the town's library.

Questions & Answers About America

At our morning prayer meetings we read the Scriptures, sang together and prayed for God to water the seed we were planting and bring forth a harvest of redeemed souls. Part of our work was answering questions from incredulous Russians whose false impressions of Americans were rapidly crumbling. Weren't Americans warmongers? Didn't they have to stand in long food lines? Wasn't the government hellbent to make war?

No one in Lavrentiya was able to learn the truth about the United States from the Voice of America or any other U.S. programs because their radios were set, by law, only to receive stations aired by the Communist government. No Christian radio station could be heard, even though the nearest one, KICY, was only a couple of hundred miles to the east.

After our devotions each morning "Siberia Mission" had gospel meetings for children. In the evenings, from 150 to 200 children were joined by adults who crowded into the Cultural Center Auditorium for our program. We gave them the Gospel of Jesus Christ in word and song and the old Cultural Hall seemed to come to life. For years it had gathered dust and accumulated cobwebs. I asked German Volnov why this place--complete with a stage and curtains and an upright piano--

had not been used for so long. He shrugged. "We have had no reason to use it," he said. "There's nothing to celebrate here."

After the last actors had left eight years earlier, the place required an enormous and expensive cleanup effort. But we Christians left the auditorium cleaner than we had found it. It was wonderful to see the gospel put sparkle in the eyes of the Russians.

We filled the auditorium by advertising nearly every hour on the hour over the town's only radio station at a cost of six cents per word! The whole town knew that Americans had come. We sang and preached to a full house for a week. Many came to see us out of curiosity; many others because their children insisted that their parents hear the Americans; others came because their hearts were empty; and still others came because they remembered missionary Dick Page, his father Don, Wally Kulakoff and others who had visited a year earlier.

Out of the brightness of His presence clouds advanced,
with hailstones and bolts of lightning.
The Lord thundered from heaven;
the voice of the Most High resounded.
He shot His arrows and scattered the enemies,
great lightning and routed them.
The valleys of the sea were exposed
and the foundations of the earth laid bare
at Your rebuke, O Lord,
at the blast of breath from Your nostrils.
He reached down from on high and took hold of me;
He drew me out of the deep waters.
He rescued me from my powerful enemy,
from my foes, who were too strong for me.
They confronted me in the day of my disaster,
but the LORD was my support.
He brought me out into a spacious place;
He rescued me because he delighted in me.

Psalm 18: 12-19

CHAPTER THREE

Men and Singing Angels

CHAPTER THREE

Men and Singing Angels

The teenagers from Soldotna had learned several Christian songs in Russian for this trip. We sang and played right along with them. Barb and I sang simple choruses and songs, the messages of which could easily be translated into Russian. Cary Dietsche played Gospel songs and hymn arrangements on his Roland 88-key piano, the likes of which our audience had never seen before. The Russians loved his playing. Don Wharton sang and played his Ovation guitar. Don and I shared simple Gospel messages, interpreted by Wally Kulakoff who ended each meeting with "summary statements" and an invitation for people to know God personally by believing in His Son, Jesus.

The people of Lavrentiya seemed eager for our message of hope. They told us they were always hoping that every plane that landed would bring good food for them to buy, to make their lives a little easier and happier. Most of the people had circles under their eyes as if they were always tired and needed a vacation. Their eyes were expressionless. They had lost a sparkle. Smiles were the exception rather than the rule. People in Lavrentiya always talked of the mainland where there were roads from one town to another, trains, buses and public transportation. They felt cut off from the rest of the world and radio was their means of knowledge. People here remembered how their parents were sent to these places because the war left many children homeless and orphans, born to people who had been sent to Lavrentiya by their government. Some still hold a grudge against the government because there is no economic way out of The Russian Far East. Even if they could leave, where would they go? Where would they live and work when they got there? On top of that, incredible inflation makes what ruples they have saved all but worthless.

In Russia, you stay where you were born because you have your residency in the city or town or village where you were born. You can only move if you are in the military, studying, or marry someone in another village. You can also move if you are in military service. All of your moves are recorded in your internal passport which is given to everyone turning 18 years of age. Russians in Lavrentiya stay there because they have nowhere else to go. They may have relatives on the mainland, but no job opportunities, no permit to live anywhere else except in the town where they were born.

The Eskimos living on the Peninsula number about 8,000. They dream of visiting their relatives in Alaska or on St. Lawrence Island. They all hope for a better life in the future, some because they have relatives in Alaska. The Chuchi Indians hate the Eskimos who number about 20,000. They want the peninsula to become independent from Russia and from the Eskimos. Chuchi Indians want to return to the old ways but alcohol has destroyed their young people and the youth are seen as lazy, fat, and unable to think for themselves.

An Orphan Finds Her Father

One day as Wally and I were walking down a street near the waterfront we met a woman walking toward us. Wally soon recognized her and called out her name. "Rosa! It's you!"

Rosa stopped, smiled at Wally and then started to laugh. They threw their arms around each other and chatted in Russian for several minutes. As we walked on, Wally turned to me and said, "Dave, I must tell you about Rosa."

At the meeting here a year ago, Wally, Dick Page, his father Don and three other Christian laymen from Alaska, invited anyone in town who wanted to meet them to come to a room in the town hall. Thirteen people came that first night. The American visitors explained that they were Christians from Soldotna, Alaska on the Kenai Peninsula. Wally explained that he was an Australian citizen living in Quito, South America, the son of Russian parents who had left ahead of Stalin's purges. Each of the team members related the story of their spiritual journey, leading to salvation in Jesus Christ and the hope of eternal life freely provided by Him. Each was a lay person whose story had great appeal to the Russians.

Wally had asked the people of Lavrentiya if anyone had any questions. Rosa had stood to her feet and said, "I have been in charge of all the anti-American activities in Lavrentiya for more than twenty-five years. I have been a member of the Communist Party all my life. I came here to disrupt this meeting. I have hated America and I have hated Americans."

Rosa cleared her throat and hurried on: "I have listened to you tonight and I understand that you are sincere in what you believe. Now, I have a question for you. You talk about a God of love. Your God can't be a God of love. A few years ago my seven-year-old grand-daughter was struck and killed by a drunk driver here in Lavrentiya. How could a God of love allow such a thing to happen? What did my little girl do to deserve such a thing?"

Wally said that the most amazing thing happened while Rosa stood there waiting for an answer. Don Page stood up and said, "I would like to answer this woman. I used to have seven children; now I have six. I had a seven-year-old daughter who was struck down by a drunk driver. I will never understand why that happened. I do know I will see her in heaven someday. I'm not mad at God because my daughter died, even though I don't understand why it happened. I do not hate God; I love God. I know his purposes are different from mine and I have learned over the years to trust in God. He knows what is best."

At that point, Don Page had stepped off the platform and walked over to Rosa who was still standing after the exchange. Don had thrown his arms around her and said, "I love you." And Rosa had wept. She had been exiled to Russia's Far East as a child because she was a cast-off orphan. Today Rosa lives a happy life, confident of her salvation, happy to be in the family of God, thankful for the missionaries from the once-hated Americans who had brought her the light.

"You 'Say' and You 'Do'"

At the start of one of the evening meetings in Lavrentiya, Cary Dietsche told the young people that his six-year-old son, Jordan, and eight-year-old daughter, Lindsay, were praying that all the boys and girls in Lavrentiya would come to know Jesus as their personal Savior.

Then the young people from Soldotna sang in Russian, "Give thanks with a grateful heart, give thanks to the Holy One, give thanks for He has given Jesus Christ, His Son...."

At the close of the service, Wally opened the Bible and explained in the Russian language the clear message of the Gospel of Jesus Christ "available to all."

After the meeting was over, the speakers stepped down from the platform and introduced themselves to as many people as possible. The ones who knew a little English asked questions about the message.

One such person was Anitoli, a pharmacy intern with whom I had become friends. Anitoli put his hands on my shoulders, looked me in the eye and struggled in his primitive English to give his appraisal of our meetings: "You 'say' and you 'do'.... It's easy to say, but hard to do. I believe what you 'say' because you 'do'."

Anitoli was referring to the fact that the missionaries had brought 1,000 pounds of medicine which was made available to his clinic and to the hospital. This bright university student had been overwhelmed by the fact that the Americans not only talked about the love of God but offered medicine free to prove the point.

At the last meeting in the theatre that wasn't used much anymore by the people of Lavrentiya, Wally was moved to ask people to raise their hands if they would like to make peace with God and accept Jesus Christ as their Savior. That night 12 people raised their hands.

Wally will always remember the woman we called the "bag lady". Here is how he tells it:

She always had several plastic and material bags in her hands with all kinds of things in them. Polished stone pebbles from the shore...pieces of ivory...wooden objects and post cards of Russia. She also had many pockets in her clothing with different powders and herbs in different pockets. She came to every meeting possible even to the hotel rooms where some of us stayed. She wanted every piece of literature we had and listened intently to everything anyone from the USA said. She was fascinated with the person of Jesus Christ and thoroughly enjoyed the picture book Bible which she read all night and she wanted to know more about Him. Upon our returning to Alaska she was at the airport with her bags and she came up to me and handed me a folded page from a writing pad and said: "Read it on the plane."

I asked her if we should one day return. She quickly nodded her head. Then I asked her what was her responsibility in the town and she quietly answered, "I am the medicine woman for the non-Russians."

Medicine woman, I thought. She told me she had powers to heal headaches, deliver people from fears, stop stomach aches, and cure fevers. She had herbs and powders to help people. She also knew chants and rhymes that would help a sick person. Then I asked her why this group of Americans were fascinating to her. She told me we were the first Americans she had seen with her own eyes; and second, she said they had something she wanted--a new power. What was that power? I asked her. She revealed to me that they had a Spirit, a Spirit which she, too, has asked to be her Spirit.

She was half Chuchi and half Eskimo. These people had only evil spirits. They appeased them, worshipped them, adored them and have developed folk-lore about them. But they had never heard of a <u>Holy</u> Spirit. This Holy Spirit was able to raise Jesus Christ from the dead and hence, He was greater than all the spirits they had. She closed her book of poems and told me, "I, too, have asked Jesus Christ to be my Savior and have asked His Holy Spirit to live in me.

A Former Atheist is Baptized

At the close of our final service, Rosa approached Wally shyly and asked if she could be baptized. Wally told me what Rosa desired to do and asked, "Can you baptize her?"

I have been active in lay ministry in The Lutheran Church for more than 30 years. I replied, "Absolutely!" There was no clergyman for several hundred miles and Rosa desired to be obedient to the Lord. "It would be an honor," I said.

"Dave," Wally added, "Rosa wants her eight-month-old grandson to be baptized as well. Can you do that?" My answer was yes.

Among the fifteen people who gathered in a side room for the service were Dick and Kathy Page, Dick's father Don whose witness had impacted Rosa's life a year earlier, Missionary Aviation Fellowship pilot Dave Olson and his wife Joanne, Barb, the group's "shadow," Little German, Cary Dietsche, Don Wharton, Brian Brasher, Rosa, and Rosa's daughter and grandson.

No running water was available, but Barb recalled seeing a one-gallon bottle of drinking water backstage which we had brought from Alaska so she retrieved it to use for baptismal water. I opened the service by explaining to Rosa the significance of baptism in the life of an adult believer, sharing instances from the Scriptures in which people who believed in Jesus were baptized. I emphasized that Rosa, through her desire to be baptized (which often led to persecution in Russia), would become one of the millions who, for the past 2,000 years, have identified themselves as followers of Jesus Christ. As I placed the water on Rosa's head in the name of the Father, the Son and the Holy Spirit, tears filled our eyes. Rosa wept as she became the first person in the history of Lavrentiya, and perhaps in the entire Chukotka Peninsula, to be baptized into the Body of Christ. It was a holy moment. A stronghold of Satan had begun to crumble because the power of Jesus is greater than the enemy's.

In the most touching baptismal service I have ever witnessed, a team member poured the water directly into my hands as I led Rosa through the service and prayed that her obedience would characterize her life for the Lord for the rest of her days.

As I took Rosa's eight-month-old grandson in my arms to baptize him into the Body of Jesus Christ, I reminded Rosa that baptism "is not magic, not some form of hocus pocus. In fact," I said, "it is faith being born in the life of a child...a faith that must be nurtured in God's Word."

This active baby, who had been passed back and forth among several adults standing in the group, looked up into my eyes and was totally at peace as I poured the water on his head. I requested prayer for Rosa and her grandson and for everyone in Lavrentiya who had come to the Lord for salvation. There was no church or Sunday school to leave behind but we hoped that one would be established soon. The good news of the Christian message had shined in the hearts of these people who have lived in darkness for so long. Our prayers are being answered. In 1994 and 1995 more than 300 children were involved in Vacation Bible Schools in both cities. Provideniya already has two evangelical gatherings in town, according to Wally Kulakoff. They meet at different times on Sunday so people can attend both services if they desire. Lavrentiya is more removed and hence a permanent work will be more difficult to establish unless a missionary is willing to live there and model by example.

We shared tears of joy, smiles and laughter while we were in Russia. We knew beyond a shadow of doubt that this was God's plan. What had just happened brought joy in heaven.

CHAPTER FOUR

Some Through the Water

CHAPTER FOUR

Some Through the Water

t mid-point during our three-day evangelistic meetings a large Russian helicopter was made available to us to transport the last of our food rationings--mostly carrots and onions--to Uelen, further north where the Bering Sea meets the Arctic Ocean. That monster machine was so huge and so noisy we had to wear ear plugs to keep from going deaf. What a scary mission.

The morning of our departure from Lavrentiya, August 13, dawned gray and windy. This was Friday, August 13, but when we crossed the International Dateline just west of the U.S. border near St. Lawrence Island, we would live again the last part of Friday the thirteenth of August. As we said goodbye to our gracious hosts and carried our luggage toward our rendezvous with the other team members at the "White House" I counted our flights: One from Nome to Provideniya, another to Lavrentiya, another to Uelen, another back to Lavrentiya from Uelen, and now three more awaited us--one to Provideniya, another to St. Lawrence Island, and then the final leg home. Seven flights. Valerie Bullocks's prophecy faded in my mind but the horror of the possibility was still there. Right or wrong, I never told my wife or any of the team members about the call from the woman who had a vision of all of us crashing into the sea and perishing. This was the time to turn our faces toward home with happy memories of lost people who had come to Christ for eternal salvation in Russia, not with fear in our hearts. In a few hours we would be in Shishmaref, a small and wonderful Eskimo village north of Nome in a Lutheran church for a scheduled concert. We loaded our equipment and baggage carefully into the beige Piper Navajo PA31/A including our sound system, a keyboard, an amplifier, transformer, 20 rolls of exposed film, and my new camera. Dave Cochran, a 70-year-old veteran pilot with 18,000 hours, had flown a

Cessna 310 to Lavrentiya the night before with medical supplies, had spent the night in Lavrentiya, and was now ready to take us back to the States.

As he filed his flight plan and checked the instruments Dave estimated that the plane had 1:30 hours of fuel left. The fuel gauges showed 1/4 full on the main tanks so he put 30 gallons into the main tanks which brought the fuel gauges to a little over the 1/2 mark. Since the fuel level cannot be seen in the fuel tanks at less than 3/4 full, he estimated on the basis of time and fuel consumption that there would be about 2:15 hours of fuel left. The flight to Nome was estimated to take 1:25 hours.

'Some Through Great Trials'

At 2 p.m. we climbed aboard our plane for the last time and buckled up. As we were strapping ourselves in, a gentle wind tugged at our ship and clouds overhead were turning black. Barb pointed with a shiver to the fuel gauges standing at what appeared to be a little under 1/2 full and I thought again of Valerie's's dreadful vision. Surely nothing could be wrong. I assured her that we were in the hands of a veteran bush pilot and that the Lord was with us. We would be back on home turf before sundown. A quick stop at Gambell on St. Lawrence Island to have our passports stamped by the person who represents the United States and then the final hop to Nome. We would be singing in Shishmaref before you knew it. My wife squeezed my hand. I knew Barb was praying.

At the last minute, our pilot put seven empty blue and white five-gallon Chevron gas cans onboard to take back to Nome so he could bring extra fuel to Lavrentiya on the next trip to Russia.

Dave started the engines. In a few minutes we were rolling, taxiing into position and then streaking down the runway at Lavrentiya, praising God for the wonderful people we had met there, and thanking Him for the trophies of His Grace. The nose came up and those powerful engines pulled us toward the sky. Our pilot banked and headed south to the point of exit at Provideniya. At mid point turbulence struck us full force, turning our plane into a bucking bronco. Barb kept her eyes fixed on the instrument panel and prayed. She tried to shake her apprehension but dark feelings of oppression persisted.

Joining us on the flight was a middle-aged Russian citizen heading back to his home in Alaska. He was asked by Russian customs officials to exit the plane at Provideniya. His countrymen determined that his passport was not in order. For nearly an hour he argued with customs agents who kept making phone calls and huddling in serious discussions. Finally the Russian informed us, "I have got to get my affairs straightened out. I may need to fly to Moscow. Sorry to have delayed you. Go on ahead without me."

We noticed that our pilot had placed in the back of the cabin 10 more blue-and-white gasoline cans with "Chevron AV Gas" painted on the sides.

Dave Cochran taxied the plane to the end of Provideniya's airport. We would be flying by IFR at 7,000 feet altitude toward "OME," (FAA code for the Nome airport), with an estimated flying time of one hour and forty-five minutes. The pilot calculated that N6SF had enough fuel in the tanks and to spare for the trip home. He turned his ship around 180 degrees at the end of the gravel runway to face east, opened its throttles and soon the seven souls onboard were racing toward the sky. I settled back and fell asleep but Barb kept watching the instrument panel and praying. Sleet attacked our plane and wind jerked it around in the sky en route to Gambell.

The Final Flight for N6SF

Twenty-five minutes later the plane wobbled down through the terrible winds to land on a lonesome runway a mile and a half from Gambell, a tiny Eskimo village on St. Lawrence Island--our official port of entry into the United States. It was Friday the thirteenth again because we had crossed the International Dateline. Gambell's runway had been built during the Cold War and was made long enough for large military airplanes. Somehow Dave got the plane leveled off for a landing. Three men on four-wheeled, all-terrain vehicles were waiting at the runway as N6SF taxied up. Dave killed the engines, slid back his window and yelled above the wind that they needed a U.S. custom's agent to stamp their passports so the three men raced away on their bikes. A few feet from N6SF sat another Piper Navajo owned by Bering Air, flight 4666 headed for Savoonga with two passengers. Pilot Terry Day was running an hour late that day--a small detail that would have enormous repercussions in the divine scheme of events now closing in on us missionaries. Barb whispered to Pam Swedberg that she was afraid the plane would tip over. *How in the world could they get off the ground in weather like this? If only those gas gauges would show full....*

The wind continued to blow as the missionaries watched for the customs agent. Their plane rocked and shivered unsteadily.

Soon the agent, Rodney Ungalik, appeared on his motorcycle in a cloud of dust. "Welcome home!" he boomed, grinning broadly.

Cary Dietsche stepped outside in the wind so that Mr. Ungalik could enter the plane, sit in his seat and stamp all the passports.

Before the agent left, I asked if he would telephone the Lutheran pastor in Shishmaref to report our difficulties in getting away at the Provideniya airport and that we would be arriving late for our concert in his village.

"No problem," Mr. Ungalik replied as he climbed out. "I'll call him right away."

Cary got back into the plane, closed the door behind him and found his seat as Dave Cochran throttled up to taxi into position for the plane's last takeoff. The engines performed flawlessly as the bird rose to its assigned altitude of 7,000 feet. Several of us dozed.

While I slept, Barb sat leaning forward in her seat, her eyes fixed on a fuel gauge that continued to edge closer to "Empty". She remembered Pam Swedberg's comment that "the flight to Nome should only take around another 45 minutes". She praised God that it would not be much longer. She began calling on God and His angels, feeling that something terrible was about to happen. At that point, I'm told, we broke through the clouds into clear, blue skies and sunshine, and Barb relaxed, keeping her eyes fixed on those gas gauges, watching them twitch lower and lower....

Suddenly the right engine coughed and she jumped. It ran for another minute then sputtered again. Calmly the pilot switched on a pump to cross-feed fuel from the left to the right engine, still convinced he had plenty onboard.

The right engine coughed again and Barb tightened her grip on the seat in front of her. The second hiccough jolted me awake in time to see the propeller on the right engine slow down, shake unsteadily then go dead. I heard the pilot radio to Nome, "Out of fuel on one tank...descending from seven thousand feet...." Barb turned her face toward heaven and wept. "If only...."

The voice of the Nome traffic controller crackled through static:
"November Six Sierra Foxtrot, are you declaring an emergency?"
"Yes...please," Dave Cochran replied.
"Say how many souls on board."
"Seven."

The pilot quickly took stock. He had filled the tanks with enough fuel and had 25 minutes to spare. In all of his 18,000 hours in the sky, nothing like this had happened. Would negligence cause our "Mission to Siberia" to end in tragedy? Had Valerie's vision been a warning from God which we should have heeded? Had I disobeyed Him by ignoring it? The memory of the vision was coldly threatening as we stared at the dead engine whose propellers were now feathered to eliminate drag. The remaining engine purred on, but in a few moments the rhythmic breathing of the Navajo's powerful left engine began to sputter intermittently. Finally it, too, was silent.

Pilot Dave Cochran glanced around at his passengers as the nose pitched forward and we stared at the angry sea. Twenty-three-year-old Brian Brasher, the youngest member of the team and occupant of the seat beside the pilot, was deep in prayer. So was everyone else. There was no panic, even though everybody onboard recognized our desperate plight. Each stared down in stunned fascination as the rolling sea rushed toward us.

This is the pilot's report:

"About 50 minutes out of Gambell I switched the right engine to the auxiliary tank, expecting about 20 minutes of operation, but the engine quit about 10 minutes later. I then switched back to the main tank and about 5 minutes later it quit. I noticed then that the fuel gauges showed 1/8 full but there was definitely no fuel. I called Anchorage Center and told them I was out of fuel on one engine and had no idea how much fuel was left on the other, and was heading for Sledge Island."

In a blur, sea and sky blended as we sank lower and lower, powerless to rise again. Suddenly the waves had encircled us. Then came the first faint jolt as the fuselage met the tops of four-foot swells. Dave's white knuckles gripped the wheel as he skillfully held the nose slightly higher than the tail. The plane's fuselage bounced on the waves as its wings cut thin slices of water off the surface at 90 miles per hour, sending a plume into the sky like a fountain. Dave struggled to keep the plane from cartwheeling, knowing that it would disintegrate quickly and sink immediately if allowed to hit the water too hard.

The pilot continues in his report leading up to the crash:

"By this time we were at 3,500 feet and holding 130 mph which is about the best glide speed I could get with both props feathered. I was mentally figuring the best way to touch down in the water, as it was obvious we were not going to make it to Sledge Island. I was looking for swells on the water but there was no pattern so I elected to land on the same heading that I was now on. I was definitely going to leave the landing gear retracted and was trying to decide whether to leave the flaps up or to put them down. Since the flaps would be the first surface to touch the water, the flaps down might cause the airplane to pitch downward, putting more stress on the structure, so I decided to leave the flaps up.

We touched down at about 90 mph and slid along perhaps 300 feet. When I saw a wave building in front of the right wing tip I tried to lift the wing over it but the wave hit the wing tip and swung the airplane sideways. It stopped and turned 180 degrees from the original heading with the nose well below the water. It then bobbed up level attitude with water bubbling up through the forward floor boards. I estimated that we had about 1 and 1/2 minutes to get out of the airplane."

God Gave a Song

Our plane struck the surface like a sledge hammer against rock. Its geyser shot heavenward like a prayer as its overstrained joints screamed, its frame sashayed like a skipped rock and its nose rose and plunged on the waves like the head of a bucking horse. The plane turned around and then it stopped and gently bobbed like a crippled bird on the surface of the waves. Without a doubt, David Cochran's expert dead-stick landing had saved the lives of all seven souls onboard by keeping the plane from being smashed to smithereens.

The seawater was surging up through the plane's floor vents faster and faster, swirling and sloshing around our feet. Don Wharton had yanked the lever of the emergency door upon impact which had sent its window sailing off outside the plane. Cary Dietsche had opened the regular exit at the same time. Barb's foot got caught underneath her seat but after a moment she pulled free and headed for the door. The pilot shouted, "Grab a gas can!"

As the pilot watched, his passengers plunged into the dark water, each tightly clinging to an empty five-gallon Chevron gas can. Some of us had two. Dark despair gnawed at us. Did anyone know where we had gone down? Had anyone seen our crash? How long could anyone remain alive in that bone-numbing water--fifteen, twenty minutes? Why weren't there life vests aboard? Why not an inflatable raft? No one had ever survived an airplane crash into the Bering Sea. In the past four years, 105 commercial fishermen had drowned in Alaska. Fourteen were related to aircraft, all "occupation related"--excluding deaths by private boating or flying. Valerie. God bless her. The vision was coming true and I had not told anyone about the vision. I was still the only person who knew what was predicted to happen!

Following the crash, Cary Dietsche had fallen on his knees. Luggage in the back of the plane struck his seat with full force, tearing it from its mounts. Everyone went out the emergency exit but Cary, who exited at the regular door over the wing holding two gas cans. As he stood on the wing, the plane continued to sink. He jumped to the roof as the plane slowly lowered itself into the sea. Don Wharton, watching from the sea, yelled for Cary to jump because the tail was about to strike him.

Two thousand feet overhead, Bering Air pilot Terry Day had left Gambell on his scheduled flight, now one hour behind schedule. Out of the corner of his eye he glimpsed a disturbance on the sea beneath him. The distinct plume of water vanished before he could blink. *Just a whale spouting,* he figured.

A few minutes later his radio was telling him that an aircraft had vanished from radar in the vicinity. The controller asked him to take a look: "Bering Air forty-six sixty-six I have an aircraft in difficulty that is attempting a landing at Sledge Island. I wonder if it might be possible for you on either a VFR or an IFR clearance to deviate over to the top of Sledge Island on your way into Nome and let me know if you can spot the aircraft on the beach or possibly establish radio contact with him on this frequency or one twenty-one point five."

I wonder, he mused. *Could that whale spouting or the splash of a whale's tail I saw eight or ten minutes ago have been that plane crash-*

ing into the sea? Day rolled his plane into a sharp wing-over to get back there in a hurry. An Eskimo woman on board holding a baby screamed because she thought the plane was falling out of the sky. Terry scanned the sea. Nothing. He flew lower and lower, circling the area where he thought he had seen the spouting of a whale about 10 minutes earlier. "We're over the approximate area but we can't see anything," Day radioed. And then Steve Flowers, one of his passengers yelled, "There's a bunch of stuff down there. Go around again."

On the second pass Steve shouted, "There's people down there!" The Eskimo, a Christian lady from Nome, began to pray at once that each of us would be rescued.

Pilot Terry Day told the Nome radio dispatcher that they had spotted survivors of the crash, but that he was running low in fuel and would have to head for Nome. Vic Olson, a pilot with Baker Aviation, was flying another Navajo plane to Shishmaref. He heard the exchange and immediately turned his plane toward Sledge Island. "I've got plenty of fuel and could take over the circling post," he broke in.

"Good," Terry responded. "I want someone right here at this spot looking at these folks or we'll never find them again if we leave."

In the frigid water of about 37 degrees we struggled to hang on to the gas cans and shouted encouragement to each other: "Barb, are you okay?" "Don, where are you?" "Cary, are you doing all right?" We called out Bible verses like, "No one, not even Satan, can snatch us from God's hands, for we are His children." We quoted Psalms and favorite verses from the Scriptures. Brian Brasher kept reminding the group of God's presence, strength and power. At one point he hollered, "God is our refuge and strength, a very present help in trouble." Later we all heard him shout, "This is the day the Lord has made, let us rejoice and be glad in it." I remember thinking, *That's the wrong verse.*

This is how Cary Dietsche remembers the fateful moment:
    "I was rescued first. The helicopter came to Brian first but he told them to get me because I was having leg cramps. I was

rescued by Randy Oles in the helicopter piloted by Eric Penttila. When the helicopters came they made such a disturbance it forced you and your can underwater. You couldn't see or breathe. Randy tapped me on the head and said, 'Let's go.' I was so numb that I couldn't help him get me into the helicopter. I did make it into the helicopter after 40 minutes in the water."

At first, the water did not seem as cold as it really was. Our body heat and clothing, plus the adrenaline and the instinct to survive, gave us a false sense of security. Hypothermia lurked, ready to shut down our breathing. But in our helplessness, things were happening high overhead, back on shore, and among our families back home. In Amery, Wisconsin, Cary's children had a hard time settling down for bed. They were troubled about their father. His wife gathered them around her for special prayer for daddy at 11 p.m.--just about the time he was crashing into the Bering Sea.

At the same time, Joanne Olson, the wife of Mission Aviation Fellowship pilot Dave Olson in Lavrentiya, was praying for our safety in our hour of need.

In Washington State, where Chicago pastor David Kyllo was on vacation, he wrote later to Barb and me that "for some reason, I picked up your newsletters instead of a few books to read when we left the house.... For two weeks, I felt led to have special prayers for my two friends in Christ, and their partners in mission. Little did I know what your experiences would be."

Jay Langton from Nome Flight Service flashed word by telephone to Evergreen Helicopters' pilot Eric Penttila who had just finished dinner with his family in Nome and was about to leave his house. After Pentilla heard about the crash he called his mechanic, Jerry Austin. These two bolted from their homes and drove to the hangar where they fired up their large 162 EH helicopter which was used primarily for food and mail deliveries to isolated villages. It was ill equipped for rescue but it would have to do. Both men expected to pick up dead bodies, but they would give it all they had. Doug Doyle, a member of the Nome Volunteer Fire Department, showed up and asked if they could use a fire fighter.

"I need the strongest, biggest man around," Penttila yelled above the engine.

Randy Oles, a tough, broad-shouldered member of the Nome Volunteer Fire Department's search-and-rescue team, grabbed seven body bags, drove to the airport and jumped in.

By this time the helicopter was fully warmed up, filled with fuel and checked for takeoff. Penttila, Austin and Oles flew like a homing pigeon twenty minutes straight to the crash site and quickly sized up the situation.

ERA pilot Walter Greaves and Dave Miles, at that moment in the air engaged in a geological survey with a magnetometer heard the airport frequency reporting that a plane was down. Greaves quickly took stock of his situation. He had an hour and a half of fuel onboard his slightly smaller helicopter owned by ERA Aviation so he offered his help.

"Come!" Penttila radioed back immediately, and so with limited fuel, Greaves and Miles unhooked the cables holding the magnetometer and headed for our site to lend a hand, even though he would be flying illegally over water. Both helicopters "just happened" to be near Nome that day.

Barb Was First to Spot

Barb was first to spot the two helicopters approaching on the horizon. She cried out to the rest of us who were drifting farther and farther apart, but by then we, too, had seen our salvation in the sky. The helicopters both had only skids instead of pontoons and neither had rescue equipment but the men aboard had plenty of dedication and determination. In a few minutes they were going to be called upon to exercise all this determination and all of their strength, and skills to somehow get down between the swells and pluck us from the grips of the unforgiving sea without letting that back rotor blade touch the water for even a second. They and we would have perished.

The flyers were shocked to find us all alive. They found Brian Brasher first. Eric Penttila lowered his chopper dangerously close to the waves so that Randy Oles could climb out onto the skid to yank Brian from the deep but he yelled that the injured Cary Dietsche needed to be picked up first. When the rescuers dragged Cary inside he was suffering severe leg cramps. His fingers, stiff from the cold, were no longer able to grasp the handles of the gas can. He was in the process of letting go of them when he was rescued.

The Evergreen crew headed next for me but I yelled for them to pick up my wife. The rescuers couldn't hear above the swirling blades and the tremendous spray of water created by them. Randy Oles again climbed out onto the skid and grabbed my hand. But my strength was gone and my clothing was soaked with seawater, giving me added weight. After several unsuccessful attempts, the skid of the helicopter momentarily dipped beneath the water and I was able to put my right leg over the skid. Oles grabbed my belt and pulled me into the ship.

Dave Cochran, the pilot, was drifting in and out of consciousness nearby. He had lost his grip on his gas can and was floating free, sinking lower and lower into the water. His heavy coat was soaked, making it difficult to pull him in. By this time the two rescuers were nearly exhausted. Both Randy Oles and Jerry Austin were outside the helicopter on the skid trying to make contact with Dave Cochran. In a final effort, they threw the ends of a rope inside to Cary and me. With what little strength we had left we pulled the rope tight and hung on. Austin and Oles slid out farther and farther on the skid, finally getting Dave Cochran in their grasp; then Penttila took off for the rock-and-tundra Sledge Island two and a half miles away. Oles and Austin literally clung to Cochran in mid-air until he was deposited on top of the island. The three men were all over that skid. When it came to rest,

Cary Dietsche and I crawled out of the helicopter and covered the 70-year-old pilot with a sleeping bag found inside as Penttila took off again to help rescue the others. Cary and I tried to give Dave a bit of warmth and make him as comfortable as possible. We had to slap his face to keep him from slipping into unconsciousness. We called out things like, "Hold on, Dave...we're going to make it...we're on top of the island...they've gone for the others."

While all of this was taking place, Terry Day of Bering Air had unloaded his passengers in Nome, refueled, and then returned to position himself in a circling pattern halfway between Nome and Sledge Island. From there he relayed information by radio from the scene to Nome.

ERA Pilot Walter Greaves and Dave Miles were having trouble plucking Barb from the water. Miles was able to grab her and keep her from sinking but her clothing was so heavy he couldn't lift her into the helicopter. She was too weak to hold on to anything and the swells made it difficult for the pilot to hover. When the waves crested and the troughs were low, the helicopter dropped closer to Barbara; when the waves fell--sometimes as much as six feet--the helicopter couldn't follow because the tail rotor might hit the wave and cause a disaster.

The frustrated rescuers were growing desperate. They finally decided to leave Barb momentarily but they couldn't bring themselves to do it. They were pretty sure she would drown because she had let go of her gas can while preparing to be raised into the helicopter. On one final, valiant try, Miles, a 30-year-old Canadian who later received the American Medal of Heroism for his efforts, hung on to a black strap anchored to the helicopter and eased himself out farther... farther... farther on the skid. He was able to grab Barbara with his free hand but then felt his grip on the strap weakening. So he let go of it and with one last mighty effort, grabbed Barbara with both hands. He locked her head between his knees and wrapped his legs around her chest as he clung to the skid.

Greaves gently lifted off the water and headed for Sledge Island, flying low above the waves as Barbara dangled beneath them. As they neared the rocky shore and began to rise to a cleared plateau seven hundred and sixty feet above the sea where the rest of us waited, the airmen were convinced that their passenger was going to escape their grip and drop on the rocks. They paused over the water a few feet from shore, and dropped Barbara back into the water.

Barbara explains:
"Oh, God!" I prayed, "help me to surface, my strength is gone." As I pushed myself upward, my breath escaped and with one final thrust toward the surface, I inhaled, my lungs filled with water. I gasped and choked in an effort to beathe the fresh air. "Let me pass into your arms of comfort", I prayed.

My dear rescuers hovered above me. Dave Miles was standing in the door of the helicopter. I cried out "Help me - help me - can't you see I'm drowning?" Frustrated and desperate in how to help, the helicopter arose and disappeared from my view.

I laid back in the water as if it were a comfortable feather bed. It somehow gave relief. I was so exhausted. I whimpered, "Jesus - Jesus - help - help." The rhythm of the plea was like a lullaby. My anxiety disappeared and God gave me an overwhelming PEACE...to die! 'You can make it! Come to me.' The voice pierced the air and I awoke from my slumbered state into full consciousness. *Was this a voice behind me?* I turned in the water. Dave Miles was standing near the rocks - in the water - 'You can make it!' I thought to myself - *have I been lying here dying all this time, and I could have walked into shore?* I placed my feet downward searching for solid ground. I stood. As I took a step forward, I fell again into the water. The hand of God had supported my stance as if to affirm His desire that I live. My courage and strength were renewed.

Barb tried her best to swim. Miles made his way toward her, shouting words of encouragement. He grabbed her and dragged her to a rock where they sat down. He massaged Barbara's trembling hands and removed her drenched coat from her shaking body to allow her clothing to absorb the heat of the sun, even though the temperature on that mid-August day was only 42 degrees.

During Barb's dramatic rescue by Greaves' helicopter, Don Wharton and Pam Swedberg, a resident of Soldotna who had joined the team for the Siberia Mission, were rescued by Penttila's team. Pam was able to get into the helicopter but Don was not. His rescuers held onto him as he dangled on the skid of the helicopter while they flew to the top of the island to join the rest of us. The island plateau was as high as a 60-story building.

Greaves made the final trip to the crash site to pick up Brian Brasher, 23, the youngest member of our team and the last to be rescued. The sun was in the pilot's eyes and he had difficulty finding Brian. There were about a dozen five gallon gas cans floating on the surface by then, scattered over 600 feet, and the Evergreen crew thought mistakenly that Brian would be with the others. His gas can was under water, making it harder to locate him. In the sea, Brian felt a surge of fear as the pilot flew over him four times without seeing him. He could have been the first to be rescued had he not insisted that the helicopters get Cary first. Greaves finally located Brian but since he was alone in the craft, he hovered over the young man until Eric Penttila and his team could return and fish Brian out of the water. The young Christian teacher was close to giving up and yielding to the effects of hypothermia because the helicopters had not returned for about 15 minutes. He had been in the water for 70 minutes. With Brian onboard, Penttila flew to the base of the island along the shore, picked up Barb and Dave Miles then delivered them to the mountain top where they joined the rest.

Penttila radioed the airport and asked for ambulances to be ready to take his wet, exhausted and trembling passengers straight to the emergency room. He needn't have bothered. The whole town was mobilized already, eager to help their "neighbors".

I was put onto corrugated metal in a freight compartment with Cary and Pam Swedberg but Cary, being claustrophobic, panicked. He had to be taken out. Dave Miles took his place. En route to Nome we struggled just to remain conscious, shivering uncontrollably.

- Pilot Cochran had managed a remarkable once-in-a-lifetime ditching in rough water to give survivors just enough time to scramble out of an intact plane.

- Seventeen empty life-saving gas cans "just happened" to be aboard.

- Air Traffic Control functioned flawlessly and coolly in an emergency, dramatically demonstrating once again the real bond that exists between controllers, pilot and passenger.

- Two choppers "just happened" to be available in the vicinity for instant dispatch to the scene. Though neither was equipped for on-the-water rescue, their presence meant the difference between life and death for seven people and they didn't stop until everyone was safe.

- Rescuer Jerry Austin acknowledged another dynamic at work. He summoned up the belief of many: "Somebody up there had to be watching over those people."

Some through the waters,
Some through the flood,
Some through the fire,
But all through the blood.
Some through great sorrow
But God gives a song.
In the night season
And all the day long.

CHAPTER FIVE

All One Body, We

CHAPTER FIVE

All One Body, We

A mbulances had raced to the airport and were waiting. The prayer rooms of churches began filling up.

Pastors Marv Eppard, Bill Welch, Jim Falsey and several other men of the cloth rushed to Norton Sound Regional Hospital where nurses, doctors and other attendants were gathered to be on hand when the victims arrived. Townspeople brought dry clothing for the survivors to use as needed. The Christian lady aboard Bering Air's Flight 4666 when the missionaries were first spotted in the water, was there too, weeping for joy and thanking God for doing the impossible. In English and in her Eskimo language she kept praying in the hospital for God to visit the missionaries with a complete recovery.

Even as the helicopters were settling on the tarmac the seven who had been just plucked from the sea were all still so cold they were shaking uncontrollably. Barbara's temperature had dropped to under 90 degrees. For that reason, and because of the large amount of salt water she had swallowed, Barb was kept overnight for extended treatment and observation. So was pilot Dave Cochran who had lost his grip on the gas can and had sunk beneath the waves when strong man Randy Oles got a rope around him and pulled him out. Once back home in Arizona, Barb and I were told by Dr. John Raife, an emergency room physician at St. Joseph's Hospital and Medical Center in Phoenix, that: "As the body loses heat, it also loses the ability to function, swim and hold the head out of the water. The biggest risk is that the swimmer becomes so cold he can no longer hold on and just gives up."

A manual entitled "Diving Medicine," published by the W.B. Saunders Company explains that...
"generalized hypothermia is the leading cause of death among ship-

wrecked survivors. The ability to recognize and treat this condition is essential. Generalized hypothermia commonly occurs in most survivors extracted from cold water. These victims are strikingly pale, frequently have generalized muscular rigidity, are shivering, and exhibit varying levels of consciousness and shock.

A specialist in preventive medicine, and a flight surgeon, Dr. David Arday, told me that we were "clearly in the 'marginal zone' of survivability out there on the Bering Sea, which begins at 15 to 30 minutes--especially given the wind and waves." The arrival of the rescue helicopters, Dr. Arday believes, provided enough stimulation to keep our adrenaline up, which helped us to maintain the will to live. It kept us conscious and kept us shivering. Believe me, we did a lot of that!

A chart we saw pegged our survivability in that frigid water at 15 to 20 minutes. Some of us had been in for 70 minutes-- more than three times that length of time. If an individual is suddenly exposed to cold water with no thermal protection, we learned, "immediate disabling effects occur. With immersion there is a sudden inspiration or 'gasping response,' which may lead to aspiration if the victim is face down." We were all very, very near the core temperature below 90 degrees F (32 C) which constitutes severe hypothermia. Some of us were minutes away from a coma and possibly cardiopulmonary arrest, which would have made us appear to be clinically dead.

The hospital staff in Nome knew all this and was ready for action when two ambulances arrived. Each of us was rushed to warm rooms, put to bed, wrapped in warm blankets and readied for examination. Two or three attendants were at every bedside. They cut off our salty clothing, massaged our limbs to restore circulation, and fed us hot beverages and food. Hypothermia had visited each of us and would have taken our lives in just a few more minutes.

As members of the press swarmed around to ask questions for their papers, one reporter was bodily removed and tempers flared for a moment but they cooled when the diplomacy of John McBride, manager of Radio Station KICY operated by the Covenant Church, prevailed. After that the press waited quietly in a staging area for detailed information about what had happened out there on the Bering Sea.

Maurice Ninham, administrator of Norton Sound Regional Hospital, had just recently read the hospital's disaster drill manual and was prepared to deal with the press. During the lengthening evening, he presented routine statements concerning the condition of the victims, and cooperated with Pastor Eppard in finding places for the survivors to spend the night when five were released. In the midst of all the activity that evening a baby girl was born.

I worked at a nurses desk scheduling flights for us all to fly to our homes in the Lower 48. Other pastors talked with us, read from the Scriptures, and encouraged us in our time of extreme trauma.

"There was a high sense of gratitude and thanksgiving," said Pastor Eppard. "When people would say, 'Boy, were they lucky,' the Christians would immediately respond, "We were blessed, protected by God through a miracle."

"Sure, we lost 'things,'" I told a reporter, "but they are replaceable. The basic message is that God provided help for us in the water, help for us through the rescuers. As God's Word says, we were 'borne up on eagles' wings.'"

What irony it was that empty gas tanks nearly killed us and empty gas cans saved our lives!

After Barbara was released, she and I were interviewed by the FAA, by the National Transportation Safety Board and by Karlin Itchoak and Nancy McGuire, reporters for *The Nome Nugget*, Alaska's oldest newspaper. They ended a long article in their September 1, 1993 edition by quoting me as follows:

"If anyone feels as if they are emotionally drowning and they are just going under, the same powerful God who rescued us and brought us back can bring people back to wholeness."

On Saturday, August 14, 1993 at 8:30 a.m., Cary, Don and Brian caught flights to their home towns in the States. Dave Cochran and Pam Swedberg returned to their homes in Soldotna, on the Kenai Peninsula. For Barb's and my trip home, Alaska Airlines rewrote our tickets, which were at the bottom of the sea and upgraded us to first class status. All the flight personnel knew what we had been through. There were a lot of tears and tender hearts as we rehearsed how different the story might have ended. As a courtesy, the pilot of our jetliner made a long turn out of Nome in the opposite direction from the usual flight plan so that he could use his special camera mounted in the cockpit to take a photograph of Sledge Island for our memory book. Looking down on what could have been our grave is an experience we will never forget.

The Navajo N6SF, still lying a hundred feet under the waves, has been replaced by Navajo 100AF, which had its engines overhauled before being thrust into service.

Eric Penttila and Walt Greaves were given the "Golden Hour Award" on February 4, 1994 by the Helicopter Association International--its highest award for heroism while flying in connection with the saving of lives in all of 1993 world wide! The ceremony took place at the Association's convention in Anaheim, California.

On August 23, 1994, the Heroism Award Ceremony drew to Nome all those who had participated in our rescue. All of our rescuers were honored by the United States Government. The brave men who were appropriately thanked and recognized at that ceremony included:

- Eric Penttila, Helicopter Pilot who rescued six of the seven
- Walt Greaves, ERA Helicopter Pilot, expert back-up pilot
- Terry Day, Bering Air pilot who located the survivors
- Vic Olson, Baker Aviation Pilot who helped keep us in view
- Dave Miles, for rescuing Barb
- Randy Oles, rescuer of Cary, our pilot, Don, Pam, Brian and me
- Jerry Austin who with Randy Oles risked his life for us
- Jay Langton, Val Larson and Jim Miller, employees of the

Federal Aviation Agency who coordinated the FAA rescue

FAA Administrator David R. Hinson flew to Nome from Washington, D.C., to present the Distinguished Service Award to Eric Penttila, Walt Greaves, Terry Day, Vic Olson, Randy Oles, and Jerry Austin.

Dave Miles, Barb's rescuer, was given the American Medal of Heroism award by Secretary of Transportation, Frederico Peña, represented in Nome by Mr. Hinson. This is the highest award given to a civilian by the United States Government and for the first time ever, it was presented to a Canadian. Dave and Kathy Miles are residents of London, Ontario.

On the day of the Award Ceremony, Barb met her rescuer for the first time since he refused to give up and found a way to get her out of the water. It was quite a meeting! She was able to ask all her accumulated questions and find out firsthand how it all had taken place.

The U.S. Government-sponsored Award Ceremony was begun and closed with prayer by the Rev. Marvin Eppard. Near the end of the meeting I was asked to speak for the rest of the survivors. "You could have rescued rock and roll or country singers," I told the group with pretended sympathy. "But it was just your luck to drag in gospel singers." Everybody laughed heartily.

I thanked God for orchestrating circumstances in which He used brave men to bring about our salvation out there on the Bering Sea. I praised all those who risked their lives to save ours and thanked them on behalf of our entire crew.

Cary Dietsche, Barb and I were invited to "entertain" the group so we sang two or three gospel songs at this government-sponsored event. The choices were entirely appropriate because everyone present seemed to acknowledge that supernatural powers had to have affected our rescue. Citizens of Nome are well aware of how quickly the Bering Sea can claim any victim who is caught in its grip. Over and over again people expressed their amazement at the "impossible" chain of events people expressed their amazement at the "impossible" chain of events which led to the survival of every passenger in that ill-fated plane.

What about Valerie's prophecy? Did it have significance? Was it a warning from God or a trick of Satan to keep us from going? When people ask me those questions I have few answers. Satan may have tried to derail the Mission to Russia but that presupposes that Satan knows the future. Most believe that God could have been testing our resolve to obey Him through our "Mission to Siberia." A community which had lived in spiritual darkness since its founding had been visited by the Light of life and wherever the cross of Christ is lifted up, Satan will actively try to keep people in darkness.

"Satan did not want the Mission to Russia to happen," a retired missionary friend wrote us. "He wanted your death to demonstrate his power to defeat goodness. But it is as though God said, 'You can crash their plane but you can't take their lives.'"

A 94-year-old friend wrote: "The prophecy came true. You did die.... Colossians 3:2-3 says, 'Set your mind on things above, not on earthly things. For you died, and your life is now hidden with Christ in God.'"

In this sense, the prediction did come true--or is coming true. I believe that the "dying to self" process is just that--a process. It doesn't happen all at once. But for me, the crash and rescue once again demonstrate the sovereignty of God. He is in control. I am not. When I give up, He doesn't. When my strength is gone, His isn't. When there is no hope, He is there.

I am a do-it-myself kind of person. I struggle with it every day. *Get it done! Make it happen. Solve the problem.* This attitude is self-sufficiency at its worst. However, the incredible circumstances in which I found myself were beyond my control. There was nothing I could do to save myself, or my wife, or my companions. I couldn't get good enough to bring about my rescue. I was helpless and hopeless.

Then came the divine rescue. To me, it is the message of the Cross demonstrated in human drama. I cannot pay for my sins; I cannot save myself; I am helpless and hopeless. Then came the cross and the unmerited rescue by Jesus.

God is a God of rescue; He demonstrated that 2,000 years ago, before that, and many times since. The Old Testament records one rescue after another. So does the New. My concordance lists the following passages:

Psalm 22:8, "Let the Lord <u>rescue</u> them...
Psalm 31:2, "...come quickly to my <u>rescue</u>...."
Psalm 69:14, "<u>rescue</u> me from the mire...."
Psalm 91:14, "I will <u>rescue</u> him, says the Lord...."
Psalm 143:9, "<u>Rescue</u> me from my enemies, O Lord."
Daniel 6:20, "...been able to <u>rescue</u> you from the lions."
Romans 7:24, "...who will <u>rescue</u> me from this body?"
Galatians 1:4, "...himself for our sins to <u>rescue</u> us...."
2 Peter 2:9, "...how to <u>rescue</u> me from my powerful enemy."
Psalm 18:17, "He <u>rescued</u> me from my powerful enemy."
Proverbs 11:8, "The righteous man is <u>rescued</u>."
Daniel 6:27, "He <u>rescues</u> and saves...."

I know a man who was rescued from homosexuality. A friend of mine was rescued from alcoholism. A person we know has been healed from the effects of child molestation. Another friend is experiencing the God of new beginnings in her new marriage. My mother-in-law was rescued from certain death by a new heart valve. And a woman we know has recently come out of an experience in a cult. Yes, God is in the rescue business.

The Bering Sea rescue is not the first one God has brought about in my life, although it was without a doubt the most dramatic. In this event He demonstrated His power and might.

My greatest fear is that I will forget the lessons to be learned...that I will take for granted God's mercy and grace. I don't want that to happen. God's grace and mercy are greater than my sins. God's power to save is greater than <u>any</u> circumstance which I might encounter. When I get in over my head, He is there to lift me up, to give me hope.

Eight months after the rescue, in a sermon at an Anchorage Lutheran Church, I told the story of God's mercy toward us on that eventful day. During the course of my message I mentioned the conversation between our pilot, Dave Cochran, and the Anchorage Air Traffic Controller who had done so much so quickly when moments counted. It was he who assigned us to the 7,000 foot altitude on the St. Lawrence Island/Nome flight and it was he who heard the pilot report the engine failure. It was the Air Traffic Controller who was quick-witted enough to get in touch immediately with Terry Day in Bering Air's Flight 4666 and ask him to look for our plane that was just lost near him. That call (1) got Terry Day to recall the splash which he thought was a whale spouting, (2) enabled Terry to return to the scene of the crash, (3) led to Terry's impossible feat of spotting us in the water, (4) reported our location to Anchorage and Nome, and (5) kept a plane over us until the helicopters were able to pull us in.

After the service a young man came up to me and said, "I guess you're destined to meet one more link in the chain."

"Who are you?" I asked as I shook his hand.

The man, Christopher Brown, grinned. "I'm the Air Traffic Controller," he said.

I hugged him and cried. Suddenly all the people around us had moist eyes from their tears as well. Later that day I visited Christopher at the Anchorage Air Traffic Control Center where he showed me around while recounting the chain of events which led him to help us at such a critical time. We owe him a lot--we, the only people ever to survive a plane crash into the Bering Sea.

I have written in my diary a dozen divine circumstances without which we would all have perished:

1. The plane did not break up upon impact as it could so easily have done.
2. 17 gas cans were onboard as our only flotation devices.
3. Terry Day was running one hour late.
4. Two, not one, helicopters were available.
5. Eric Penttila was almost gone from his home when contacted by the FAA.
6. The Anchorage Air Traffic Controller realized Terry Days' position and flight pattern immediately.
7. The winds were 20 knots out of the northwest; almost every other day in the summer they are from the southwest. If they had been blowing as usual, the wave action would have been such that we could not have been rescued. (The word of FAA)
8. Sledge Island was only 2 and 1/2 miles away. The helicopters could not have made it to Nome and had time to return for a second and third trip.
9. The tail of the plane splashed like a whale's tail, and caught Terry Day's attention.
10. A second spotter was needed aloft and Vic Olson, with plenty of fuel onboard, volunteered.
11. Everyone was able to get out of the plane in 30 seconds.
12. We all lived beyond "the limit" by two, three, and four times.

He who dwells in the shelter of the Most High will rest in the shadow of the Almighty.
I will say of the LORD, "He is my refuge and my fortress, my God, in whom I trust."
Surely He will save you from the fowler's snare and from the deadly pestilence.
He will cover you with His feathers, and under His wings you will find refuge;
His faithfulness will be your shield and rampart.
You will not fear the terror of night, nor the arrow that flies by day, nor the pestilence
that stalks in the darkness, nor the plague that destroys at midday.
A thousand may fall at your side, ten thousand at your right hand,
but it will not come near you.
You will only observe with your eyes and see the punishment of the wicked.
If you make the Most High your dwelling - even the LORD, who is my refuge -
then no harm will be fall you, no disaster will come near your tent.
For He will command His angels concerning you to guard you in all your ways;
they will lift you up in their hands, so that you will not strike your foot against a stone.
You will tread upon the lion and the cobra;
you will trample the great lion and the serpent.
"Because he loves me," says the LORD, "I will rescue him; I will protect him,
for he acknowledges my name.
He will call upon me, and I will answer him; I will be with him in trouble,
I will deliver him and honor him.
With long life will I satisfy him and show him my salvation."

Psalms 91

CHAPTER SIX

'His Truth is Marching On'

*C*HAPTER SIX

'*His Truth is Marching On*'

God is quietly working in the hearts of people living on the Chikotka Peninsula. In the summers of 1994 and 1995, an average of 300 Russian children in Lavrentiya and Provideniya took part in two weeks of Vacation Bible School activities. Short-term teaching visits by American pastors have resulted in the establishment of a nucleus of baptized Christians there.

Plans for the developing of a church in Lavrentiya revolve around identifying and training a local pastor whom God will raise up to become the spiritual leader.

The Church of Lavrentiya can serve as the hub of mission activities throughout the Chikotka Peninsula where people will find hope through Christ our Lord. I'm happy that the Lord let us live to see it.

Expressions of loving concern began to come from hundreds of friends who gave God the glory with us for His deliverance. In a thousand letters and through phone calls, faxes and personal encounters, our friends offered encouragement and support, as well as gifts for the replacement of all our equipment:

- "We were very surprised and very happy to hear of your miraculous deliverance! Sometimes I wonder why God chooses to go to such great lengths to demonstrate His grace." --Larry and Donna Troxel, Quincy, Illinois

- "Hallelujah! Praise God! Thank you, Lord, for saving these two servants and their helpers from the jaws of death. Wow! Whew! God will use it to bless your buttons off and thousands of people."Pastor Bill Vaswig, Bellevue, Washington.

- "What an incredible story of the power of prayer and the work of the Holy Spirit to stir up intercessors for you at the time of peril! Your story is an excellent example of how God keeps Christian leaders in times of danger and preserves their ministries in answer to the prayers of others.... I am reminded again of God's faithfulness: 'All things work together for good for those who love Him.'"--Pastor Steve Wagner, Carrollton, Texas.

- "The Bering Sea is off-limits for swimmers. Try a swimming pool in Phoenix--a shallow one. God bless you...and He did."-Violet Nelson, Kingman, Arizona.

- We like the way fellow crash survivor, Don Wharton, put it:

> God has provided,
> And He has decided
> The "Gas Can Seven"
> Ain't goin' to Heaven *today!*

- "The elements in Alaska can be very unforgiving, and happy endings are always a cause for celebration. Alaskans are a hardy bunch, and their can-do attitude has proven once again to be the element needed in a pinch. We are also looking into awarding the men involved the Medal of Heroism. The criteria are very strict and only 29 have received it since its inception in 1965."-Alaska Governor Walter J. Hickel (He enclosed copies of commendations and letters from him to the pilots, rescuers, Nome Volunteer Search and Rescue, Norton Sound Medical Center and the visiting pastors, praising them for their outstanding efforts on our behalf.)

Many unanswered questions remain. We won't know all the answers until we see the Lord face to face. But we have learned again that God has a purpose for our lives and our ministry. All we could do was lift a hand--and a very weak one at that!

Just as God plucked us from our drowning, near-death experience in Alaska, He can rescue other people from dire circumstances in which they are drowning. God's power is available to them as it was to us. Praise the Lord!

Are you drowning in overwhelming circumstances? Do you feel as though there is no hope, that your situation is out of control? Well, it may be out of your control, but not out of God's control.

The message of a song I sing says, "He is able to rescue you. He understands your need. He can heal your heart and pain...give you hope again. He is able; He is able."

When I get to heaven, I'm going to look up Shadrach, Meshach and Abednego. They, too, were in an impossible situation. Even the unbelieving King Nebuchadnezzar could see the reality of God's power by rescuing them from death in the midst of the fiery furnace. After the king called his three prisoners out of the furnace he said, "Praise be to the God of Shadrach, Meshach and Abednego for rescuing His servants."

Speaking for all the survivors of the crash, it is my prayer that doubters and unbelievers will see the presence and power of Almighty God in all of this drama. It is His story, not ours.

If I can help you to believe for the first time, or to renew your faith, write to me at:

The Fellowship Ministries
6202 S. Maple
Tempe, Arizona 85283

I can do everything through Him who gives me strength.

Philippians 4:13

Photos

'Scrapbook'

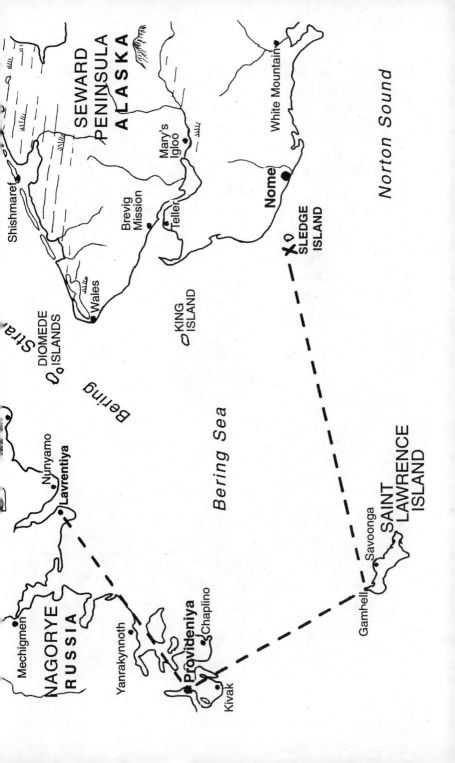

(left to right top row) Jay Langston, Walt Greaves, Dave Miles, Randy Oles, Jerry Austin, Val Larson, Jim Miller
(left to right bottom row) Dave Cochran, Cary Dietsche, Brian Brasher, Terry Day, Eric Penttila, Vic Olson, Barb Anderson, Dave Anderson
(not pictured: Don Wharton and Pam Swedberg)

The town of Lavrentiya: (left to right) hospital, most other buildings are apartments. See power plants off in the distance.

The original all terrain vehicle in Lavrentiya.

Weighing the coat Barb was wearing in the Bering Sea.
Wet: 50 lbs; dry 7 lbs!!

*Current "Road Manager",
Raymie Gunning with VBS
children in Provideniya ,
June '94.*

*The famous Sledge Island
(Old English for sled),
named by Captain James
Cook. It is 760 feet high,
covered with rocks and
tundra. The Alaska
shoreline is in the
background.*

*(Left to Right)
Dave, ERA Captain Walt
Greaves, Barb, and Dave
Miles. Captain Greaves
piloted Barb's rescue
helicopter.*

Barb and her rescuer, Dave Miles on the day of "The Heroism Award Ceremony", Nome, Alaska

Dave with the City Hall "Guard", to whom Barb gave the Bible to in '93.

Lavrentiya's Elementary School.

Lavrentiya, with the airstrip in the center.

The Provideniya airport. "Our plane" is in the background closest to the terminal.

Heros Walt Greaves and Eric Penttila, receiving "Golden Hour Award, the highest award given by the Helicopter Association International, nominated by the survivors.

On a 1994 flight back to Russia... making sure there is enough fuel.

A 50-60 year old house in Provideniya.

Russian helicopter which we flew from Uelen to Lavrentiya.

Salt water damaged photo of Cary Dietsche, Barb Anderson, Don Wharton, Brian Brasher, and the plane which we crashed.

Dave handing out God's word written in Russian.

Cary, Dave, and Barb with Soldotna, Alaska youth in the background.

Cary Dietsche, Brian Brasher carrying onions, Don Page, and Dave Olson.

Rosa and her grandson who are now new Christians.

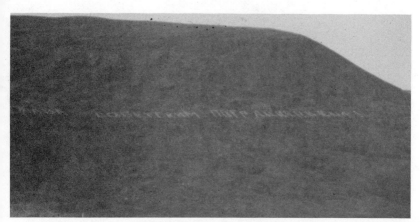

On a hill near Provideniya spelled out in stones: "Glory to the Russian Border Guards".

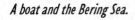

A boat and the Bering Sea.

The town of Lavrentiya.

*Dave and Don Page
helping unload the plane.*

Lavrentiya's main street.

*Dave and "Little
German", a new believer.*

On our way from the plane, past the "department store" (first building on the left) to the White House (tall building) where we were given a room to store supplies food, medicine, instruments, etc.

(left) Barb with our hostess, Marguerite. On the table is a seal-skin coat which she handmade, blueberries from the tundra, tea, and caviar in the bowl which is common food in the Russian Far East.

Barb with a young friend.

Our "followers" with Don Wharton, Brian Brasher (top center), and Rosa and her grandson (left corner)

Don Page, Wally Kulakoff, and new believer Rosa.

Anitoli with Dave.

Don Wharton gets support from Warren Little and Randy Oles of Nome Search and Rescue.

Orthodox crosses have begun to appear in Provideniya cemetery

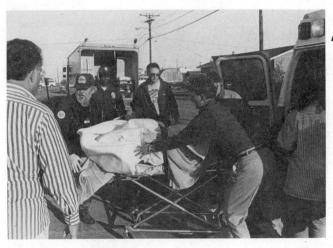

Dave Cochran being transported to Norton Sound Regional Medical Center by the Nome Emergency Medical Unit.

(below) Nome rescue personnel prepare to transport Pilot Dave Cochran to Norton Sound Regional Medical Center.

(below) Brian Brasher gets assistance from Randy Oles and Matt Johnson.

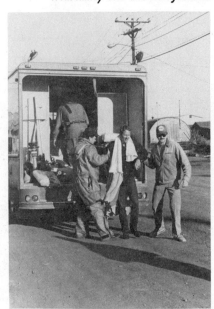

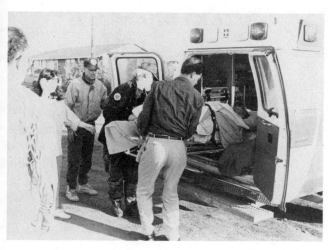

Nome emergency personnel transport Barb to Norton Sound Regional Medical Center after her hypothermia experience in the Bering Sea.

Kevin Ahl assists Cary Dietsche along with Randy Oles to Norton Sound Regional Medical Center

above) Volunteer EMT Terry Wilson escorts Dave Anderson to the emergency vehicle.

 *RITERS BIOGRAPHY*

*N*orm Rohrer is the Founder and Director of the Christian Writers Guild. He is the former Editor of World Vision Magazine, past Executive Secretary of the Evangelical Press Association, and former Director of the EP News Service.

Norm has published more than 1,000 feature articles and news stories in more than 175 periodicals. He has written 25 published books for five publishing houses.

Married to Virginia, the Rohrers make their home in Hume Lake, California.

*D*ave Anderson is the President of The Fellowship Ministries, Tempe, Arizona. Since 1963 he has been active in youth, worship, and music ministry within the Lutheran denomination. He is the founder of Lutheran Youth Encounter, Lutheran Youth Alive, Renewal House, and several other organizations.

Since 1975, he and his wife Barbara have been engaged in concert ministry throughout the United States and abroad. Dave is compiler of The Other Songbook and publisher of the Worship Leaders' Resource Magazine. Previous works have been published by Augsburg Publishing House and Concordia Publishing House. Dave and Barb Anderson make their home in Phoenix, Arizona.

r